PUSHPENDRA MEHTA

OBSERVE

— to —

UNMASK

100 SMALL THINGS
TO KNOW PEOPLE BETTER

Observe to Unmask by Pushpendra Mehta

Published in the United States by Kindle Direct Publishing.

Edited by Elizabeth Barrett

ISBN 979-8653727696

To:

God, for the gift of writing, intuition, and reflection you so graciously blessed me with.

The British author Sir Arthur Conan Doyle, for combining his love of science and literature to create the memorable fictional detective character, Sherlock Holmes, that influenced me to observe human behavior carefully and to blend my love for writing and self-discovery.

"Pursue your passion, work with your intuition, learn as a child, and adapt as water."

—Pushpendra Mehta,
The Suitable Inheritor

CONTENTS

INTRODUCTION

In March 2019, when I answered a question—"What small thing can tell you a lot about a person?"—that was posted on Quora, a popular question-and-answer website, little did I realize that my answer would get over 1 million views. This was attained without any paid advertising on my part.

Spurred by the engaging response, I decided to expand on my answer and create a short book that would serve as an instant reference to help readers observe the small yet important things to know people, including themselves, better, and to benefit from these insights for a happier and more fulfilling life.

For as long as I can remember, I have been an observer. Perhaps because I was raised to notice the minutest aspects of life, I started to observe people, their mindsets, their subtle emotions and feelings, as much as I watched myself, my frailties, ego trips, and inward and outward journeys.

I was also influenced by Sir Arthur Conan Doyle's

famed fictional detective character, Sherlock Holmes. Some of Doyle's books on Holmes led me to believe that human behavior is remarkably complicated and there is much to be discovered about people. So "observe and notice" became my credo to understand and uncover people in my mind. In time, this would sharpen my ability to draw conclusions quickly and accurately from the smallest observations.

I was always a sensitive person. That explains why I am a writer, storyteller, marketer, and mentor. If you cannot *feel deeply*, you cannot write, create content, narrate stories, promote services, and provide advice or guidance that resonates with the intended audience.

Observation is a solitary activity. I speak less, query more, and listen intently. This helps me notice more and know better the people I interact or associate with, regardless of what they share or discuss with me. It also enhances awareness of my own thoughts and feelings.

Through the years, I learned to train myself to get into people's minds to understand the obvious, the unspoken, or the concealed, which is more an exercise to know closely their character, personality, temperament, interests, strengths, weaknesses, and, perhaps, to get a glimpse of their future. And so I have, through trial and error, practice, the ups and downs of life, my exposure to the East and the West, and my interaction with the privileged and the underprivileged, gotten better at reading people. This has facilitated the creation of this quick-read book to highlight the small things that can help you know someone better. These are small because you really have to *notice carefully* in order to see them.

Most of us wear a mask, a social mask to hide who we really are and what we're feeling, to protect ourselves, to avoid conflicts, or to masquerade a personality trait that wouldn't otherwise be appreciated or accepted. The fear that the world is going to find us out leads us to adorn a mask. This displays us in the best possible light—giving, kind, confident, secure, and humble.

We may pretend we have it all together, that everything is perfect, but the mask has cracks in it. By being more observant and aware, we can read people, not just what they say, but who they are. We can see past their masks to the real person. Remember, behind every social mask is a story.

Most of us have four sides to our personality. One we keep hidden inside. The second is what we show our immediate family, partner, best friend, and household staff. The third is exhibited in front of extended family, close friends, peers, colleagues, and coworkers; and the fourth is presented to the rest of the world. This makes it difficult to truly know what is in someone's mind and heart. But people communicate through words, silence, feelings, vibes, motives, appearances, and more.

Observe to Unmask attempts to uncover different aspects of human emotions and behavior that will help you develop relationships or associations that work for you; that assist you in comprehending an individual's backstory; prevent you from being exploited, abused, manipulated, or lied to; make you more self-aware of your own blind spots and overcome them; and aid you in distancing yourself from certain harmful people, or avoiding them as much as possible.

Observe to Unmask is based on my understanding from the school of hard knocks and the resultant game of life and relationships, including extensive reading, questioning, conversations, and listening. I like to analyze people and their interests, beliefs, preferences, struggles and failures, accomplishments and accolades, choices in words and communication styles, the circumstances that made them become who they are today, and the reasons that led them to make certain choices or decisions.

This book is not backed by data or scientific evidence. It is based on my experience and intuitive insights. You are welcome to accept, condone, reject, or condemn my observations. I am not a know-it-all, and I don't claim that my observations and experiences are superior to yours or can't be different from yours. I can only urge you to read *Observe to Unmask* with an open mind and test each of its one hundred insights to arrive at your own conclusion.

We all have an ego. When I introspected on my ego and had an honest conversation with myself, I realized this book has come to fruition largely because at some point in time, I have been guilty of being arrogant, insensitive, inconsiderate, insecure, and superficial. I have had my failures, I have made poor choices, I have made judgment errors, and I have had my anxious or uncertain moments.

In equal measure, a number of insights in this book have come about because of my penchant for risk-taking, continual experiments, and my learning and change. All of this has been fraught with pain, triumphs, reflection, and reform. Also, what helped me put this book together is a career that embraced diverse experiences and opportunities to develop, wherein I have spent years studying leaders, consultants, gurus, and entrepreneurs, trying to discern what made them become the person they are today.

Questions fuel curiosity and impel us to seek insights about human nature: Who is the best person to ask for advice? Does a person's group of friends define who he or she is? Does money matter, or is it the root of all evil? Is a person attention seeking or paying attention? How do we identify an authentic spiritual guru? Insights into these questions and more find their way into the book.

It may appear that this book is about identifying egoists and egotists, or the perfect person. It isn't so. The book is not directed toward a particular person. Its aim is to encourage self-observation, because *to observe* means to *first* observe yourself and then observe others. This will help you effectively unmask your ego, and also make you more sensitive to the feelings, emotions, and thoughts of the people around you.

If *Observe to Unmask* can help you know yourself and others better, facilitate acceptance of diverse perspectives, or assist you in making more informed choices, then the purpose of this book will have been served.

Pushpendra Mehta

1

WHAT WE LACK, WE PURSUE

1.   Denial heightens the desire.

What we lack, we pursue. What people lack in their first eighteen to twenty-one years is what they go after all their lives.

If they didn't grow up with money, then you will see them acquire (or want to obtain) big or lavish homes, luxury cars, high-end jewelry, expensive clothing, iconic handbags, and costly watches; and pursue a high-status or glamorous lifestyle for the larger part of their adult life.

If they didn't get love, attention, importance, or social validation; didn't find happiness or peace; or if a certain emotional need went unfulfilled, they will continue to search for it until they find it and feel satisfied.

Examine, observe, or study the first eighteen to twenty-one years of a person's life, and you will gain a lot of insights about the individual. Most of what was unavailable or denied to us from childhood through adulthood is what we chase for the larger part of our lives. Remember, what we lack is what we pursue, and what we lack is what we are today.

Denial heightens the desire. An individual's response to denial of material pleasures, social status, love, belonging, security, autonomy, happiness, attention, approval, or appreciation during the journey from childhood to adulthood is the key to understanding human behavior.

Gather as much information as you can about the early years of a person's life and you will know why they are what they are today, including the reasons for their insecurities and anxieties.

2

CURIOUS TO GROW OR GOSSIP?

2.   The compulsive gossiper is consistent.

If a person is a *compulsive* gossiper, know that if he or she gossips *to* you, they will also gossip *about* you.

How they speak of others to you tells you a lot about how they speak of you to others. If they share others' secrets with you, chances are they will share your secrets with other people as well.

Habitual gossipers are usually negative or toxic people who seek to exert power and control over you. They are privy to sensitive information about your personal life that can be disclosed to others to hurt you or your family's personal or professional well-being and reputation.

3. They ask questions to gossip or to grow.

Observe if they ask questions to gossip or to learn and grow. Interesting and intelligent people ask questions to spark great conversations, stay curious, and enhance their learning, or because they're genuinely interested in getting to know someone.

Gossipers query to seek out confidential information about your personal matters so they can spew it out to others. They are fueled by an insatiable need to feel important and to be viewed as people in the know. (Knowledge is power, and that makes them the go-to person).

Observe how they talk behind someone's back. If they appear friendly, respectful, or pleasant to your face, but judge harshly, criticize, act like a talebearer, or divulge sensitive information about someone when that person isn't around, know that they can't be trusted and keep them at arm's length.

If they ask questions to gather information they need and love to reveal it to others in the name of concern, care, or worry, know that they cannot stomach secrets, and it is best to keep a reasonable distance from them.

4. They *primarily* discuss ideas, events, or people.

Observe the conversations people engage in. If a person *primarily* likes to discuss ideas or offer solutions, asks questions out of curiosity to learn and grow, or immerses in purposeful, inspirational, engaging, or intelligent conversations, then he or she is an insightful, interesting, evolved individual.

If a person *for the most part* likes to discuss people (gossip) and their lives (especially their shortcomings), then he or she is more of a shallow or superficial person. And if you find a person *mostly* discussing news events happening around the world or events they did not witness or experience, know that they are more talk and less action oriented; and they are simply providing their opinion on information or facts that are already known. Such people's deliberations are focused more on issues and problems rather than on finding solutions.

5. The friends they hang out with.

Observe the friends people spend the most time with, and you will know a lot about them.

We become who we most associate with. The socialite will hang out with friends that enjoy glamorous lives and material trappings; the gossiper will socialize with news-monger friends and revel in the exchange of information or in spreading rumors; the curious, the optimist, and the bibliophile will befriend those who are interested in intelligent conversation; the spiritual seeker will associate with those who are walking a path of self-discovery, or enjoy discussing inner growth and wisdom.

Watch the friends that people hang out with and their conversations. Remember, the company they keep, the group of people they like to surround themselves with, will influence them and shape who they are. Sooner than later, we absorb the characteristics or character traits of the people we associate with, and that is what we become.

6. They gossip because deep inside, they are envious.

Gossiping is a convenient way to pour out baseless stories or tittle-tattle, but is really a veneer for envy. It is an unpalatable way to disguise envy or resentment.

Envy can come in various forms: material possessions, fame, appearance, achievements, happiness, attention, respect, intelligence, knowledge, or likeability. Envy is the acknowledgment of feeling inferior to another person who possesses something we value or desire. Remember, serial gossipers do not make loyal and trustworthy friends because they live with a sense of inadequacy and can't be happy when things are going great for you.

3

OUR SOCIAL MEDIA POSTS
REVEAL WHO WE ARE

7.   Social media is a reflection of who we are.

Social media is a reservoir of what we think, what we believe, what scares us, what we fight for, and what we approve or disapprove of.

People reveal their inner selves on social media despite attempts to shade the truth. To figure out a person, review his or her social media accounts and posts. This is their media mouthpiece and medium for self-expression. In a digital world, this is one of the most effective ways to find out who someone really is.

If *most* of what they post revolves around selfies and videos or images of themselves and their families' and friends' celebrations, hobbies, projects, and attainments, or their participation in social activities, including luxury travel pictures and stories, they are most inter-ested in sharing their lives and social networking; promoting themselves and their family (they are com-petitive people); clamoring for attention, recognition, and the validation of others. Doing so incessantly means it's more an exercise to garner publicity.

If a lot of the content they post or create is funny, creative, inspirational, helpful, purposeful, compassion-ate, or spiritual, or promotes philanthropic causes and environmental protection, that delineates their desire to make a difference.

If the larger part of their social sharing and com-menting centers on political, cultural, religious, technological, financial, or topical stories, that depicts their need to air their opinions and enhance awareness about issues that interest or affect them, their family, or the world around them.

You can also know more about people by observ-ing the groups, businesses, or celebrities they like or follow; their favorite books, TV shows, and movies; and the banter and arguments they've gotten into on social media.

Social media analysis offers accurate insights into who we are. A person's social media feed is a mirror that reflects their true self, as long as you know how to uncover the mask that people wear, showing others the best version of themselves.

4

ATTENTION SEEKING OR PAYING ATTENTION?

8.   Everything must revolve around them.

Do you know people who think the world revolves around them? Such people want the focus to be always on them. Somehow, they always circle back to their story. They crave excessive attention and admiration, as if they want to be worshiped and adored. It makes them feel worthy. When the attention is not on them, they have a faraway look in their eyes and they get impatient. Everything must flow through them because they have to be in control. These people have fragile egos and aren't good listeners.

Emotional abandonment, neglect, loneliness, desertion, and enmeshment (weak or absent boundaries between a parent and a child, or between spouses, or within whole families) form their backstory. This explains why deep down they feel inferior, insecure, flawed, or inadequate, and have an exaggerated need for validation and attention.

To compensate for the feeling of inadequacy or inferiority they live with, these people like to exude superiority over others-intelligence, popularity, beauty, generosity, charm, or goodness. They will also go as far as making a show of humility in public, which is another way to garner attention and display their superiority over others. Usually such people don't have *close* friends. They may have friends (the friends they say they have are more like acquaintances), but they struggle to form deep and intimate relationships.

9. The benevolence or charity braggart.

The person who *brags* about his or her good deeds or acts of benevolence, or talks *fervently* about the money he or she has donated to charity, or the time or expertise they offered for a noble cause, is more concerned about eliciting attention and enhancing his or her reputation with the world around them.

They may be caring, compassionate, and sensitive by nature; and their social media marketing or messaging may set an example for society to emulate in ways that may be pertinent; but their *boasting* and *advertising* of their giving (money, time, advice, or expertise) is primarily done to get praise and recognition, and to make them look better or feel better about themselves.

10. They monopolize conversations.

People who like to dominate a conversation (including a group conversation), who just won't stop talking, and who like to talk over others (chronic interrupter) have a deep longing to be heard, really heard. Their desire for self-expression and attention is intense, indicating they feel attention deprived. They treat conversation as a competition (Who gets the most airtime?), so they squelch other perspectives—and may not realize it is rude or abrasive to do so. They struggle to contain their impatience when others talk, and seek to assert superiority by taking control of the conversation. These people are smart, and their brain works much faster than many others, but they are prone to anxiety.

11. Active listening is more than just paying attention.

Observe how people listen, attentively or inattentively? Do they make consistent eye contact? Does it feel as if, even though they appear to be listening to you, they are actually distracted or bored? Do they like to share and then listen, or do they prefer talking to listening?

You can tell a good listener from a bad listener. An

active listener will inevitably show their curiosity by asking questions, encouraging other people to talk, nodding (this may vary according to cultural context), and not interrupting others. They remember what was said and respond appropriately and thoughtfully.

The poor listener will appear distracted (for instance, checking his or her phone while someone else is talking), avoid eye contact, talk excessively or monopolize a conversation, and interrupt frequently. They will ignore what they don't understand or what they don't *want* to understand, and rush others to finish what they're saying.

And so you know, good hearing doesn't mean you're a good listener, being well-read doesn't mean you're an incredible listener, and the older you get and the more experience you have doesn't translate into becoming a better listener.

12. The conversation hog.

Observe which people like being the center of attention by talking about themselves ad nauseam, showing little curiosity about what others have to offer. This leads to unhealthy conversations as these people focus on themselves, or their family's accomplishments, or topics that interest *them*. Such an attitude speaks to a lack of reciprocity and a genuine interest in others, who are confined to the role of a forced or drained listener.

At first, people like this seem companionable, a

good conversationalist, and appear to have a likeable personality. However, soon you realize they simply enjoy hearing themselves talk. Such people are conversation hogs—"Everything is really all about me, so I hog every conversation." These folks have an exaggerated sense of self-importance and continually crave approval.

When you talk to someone and start relaying your story or opinion, and the other person jumps in and brings the conversation back to him or herself, know that every conversation (and it isn't even a conversation) will revolve around them. They may also tell you the same stories over and over again, or have an opinion about everything, even if they know little or nothing about it whatever they're talking about. It's like listening to a boring monologue, and this behavior exhibits a great need to be heard.

Remember, it's all about them and not you. They aren't all that interested in you; they are interested in themselves. At the core is egocentrism.

5

DOES MONEY MATTER OR IS IT THE ROOT OF ALL EVIL?

13. Things people say about money.

Many people like, or even love, money and the material comforts it provides, and also believe that the power of money can be leveraged to make a difference in various aspects of human life: alleviating poverty; improving education; fostering creativity, innovation, and entrepreneurship; food procurement; water resource management; clean energy; and health care. Yet, many despise money because they think it is the root of all evil. If so, then why do nonprofits need capital to carry out their goal of making the world a better place to live? Why do several spiritual gurus charge a fee for their courses or sermons?

Observe what people feel or think about money, and

you will know the category they belong to: *the sour grapes, the satiated, the experience driven, and the minimalist.*

The *sour grapes* are people who couldn't make as much money they wanted to, and they cover their inability to do so by blaming money for all evils in our society.

The *satiated* are the wealthy who have experienced the pros and cons of more-than-adequate money, and the luxuries or comforts that accompany it. They are in a convincing position to comment about what money can or cannot do.

The *experience driven,* who choose experiences over material objects (the experience economy), require money for travel, investing in their passions, or the pursuit of self-discovery. Just because they don't buy designer bags, expensive homes, or luxury cars or watches doesn't mean they don't require sufficient money to experience life to the fullest. Do you think they can experience life in the way they want without money?

You can experience the marvels of nature and its five elements (fire, water, earth, air, and space) without money, but to experience the splendor of nature in another city or country, you need to travel, and is that possible without money? Is money not important?

The *minimalist,* who has actively pared his or her life down as much as possible, also requires some money, even if it is only enough cash that enables them to lead a simple and meaningful life, or achieve their objectives. Can they do without money?

Now watch those people who say money isn't important in life… they are not telling the whole truth. The extent of the fib depends on the person's state of mind. Is he or she the sour grapes, the satiated, the experience driven, or the minimalist?

There is a sole exception here: the *profound* or the *authentic spiritual* person who is in harmony with the inner and the outer universes, and who can willingly embrace adverse circumstances or live in unfavorable conditions, where money is just a means of subsistence and facilitates self-dependence or self-reliance. They know that money isn't unimportant, bad, or the root of all evil. It is *the greed behind money that is the root of all evil*, the greed-laden pursuit of wealth and power that is to blame for unfulfilled happiness.

6

GIVING AND TAKING ADVICE

14. They give the best advice.

The person who gives the best or the greatest advice is usually the one who has been through a lot. These people have turned their setbacks, obstacles, and wounds into opportunities for comebacks, for growth and change; and to reach new understandings, or epiphanies, about life, their careers, their relationships, and the people around them.

The fact that they went through a lot and evolved is what separates the *outstanding* advice-givers from those who *believe* they give great advice.

People who offer excellent advice to you today sought advice from experienced or sagacious mentors, gurus, coaches, or entrepreneurs in some capacity in the past, to adopt some of the greatest lessons of their lives and careers. In doing so, they demonstrate that they are adaptable, broad-minded, resourceful, reflective, and open to opportunity, learning, and change.

15. The advice mongers love to offer advice.

Observe how family members or friends offer advice to others—unsolicited or solicited. If they offer advice only when asked, they are generally the nonintrusive or easygoing type of person. If they love to offer advice (gratuitously) when *not* asked, these advice mongers are invariably people who like to dominate or be in control. Such advice-givers reveal a strong impulse to advise others, but aren't open to accepting advice from others.

16. They don't follow their own advice.

Before you take advice from a well-intentioned family member, friend, peer, or colleague, observe if they walk the walk. Do they *follow* the advice they give to others? Or do they give advice that they don't follow?

If their actions and words don't align, they are more preachers than doers. These inveterate advice-givers believe they are more superior in intelligence, knowledge, and comprehension than you. Outwardly, such people are authoritative and competitive, but below the surface they're much *less* self-confident and secure than you might imagine, and are looking for constant reassurance or validation.

7

HUMAN BEHAVIOR AND EMOTIONS

17. This is how you get to know someone really well.

If you want to know a person really well, get the honest opinion of his or her parents, grandparents, children, siblings, spouse or partner—or ex-spouse or partner—best friend, household staff, executive assistant, or former friends.

18. Love is a powerful emotion that overrides rational thought.

Know that a person in love is in the grip of one of the most powerful emotions, when rational thought will not work, and he or she is developing intense feelings they cannot control.

Under the overpowering force of love and deep

attachment, many make choices of partners they cannot logically explain. You will observe someone who is the best judge of people or a good judge of character make the wrong relationship choices. You can try persuasion, pressure, manipulation, or tact to dissuade them from doing so, or point out a serious red flag about their relationship, but chances are none of this will work. Remember, love defies logic and overwhelming emotions cloud judgment.

19. Your sense of humor reveals your backstory.

We use humor for different reasons. Our sense of humor says a lot about who we are, and the jokes we crack reveal our backstory.

Some people have such a terrific sense of humor, they barely have to open their mouths and you break out in uncontrollable laughter. You laugh so hard, your stomach hurts and you have tears in your eyes. You beg them to pause for a few seconds so you can catch your breath. Such incorrigibly hilarious people embody free-spiritedness with an uncanny ability to laugh at themselves. In essence, they are witty, good-natured, creative, optimistic, inquisitive (open to new experiences), and mischievous—yet they also crave attention, approval, and affection, probably because their childhood or adult life has been marked by loneliness, pain, deprivation, depression, or anxiety.

Then there is the person who humors you with wordplay or puns. They love words, and like to engage in intellectual conversations in order to stimulate their minds. Often such people are highly articulate.

From the family of humor comes another type—the sarcastic or caustic humor. No matter what the topic of conversation, a person who practices this type of humor will make a sharp or cutting utterance designed to ridicule, criticize, or hurt the listener, sometimes leaving him or her speechless.

While such people are intelligent and insightful, they offend others, aiming to erode their self-respect with biting repartee. These people carry a deep pain or frustration that needs an outlet, and it comes out through satirical wit. One of the coverups they commonly use is, "I was only kidding" or "Just kidding." They feel better about themselves by putting other people down.

20. When they come to you for advice.

Know that most people who come to you for advice don't really want your counsel.

While you may believe they have sincerely come to you for advice because they respect you for your wisdom or good judgment, they really want praise, validation, or support. They want to hear their ideas or preferences confirmed by an experienced person or expert. They want you to tell them what they want to hear. They don't want the truth, they just want your approval.

The general *exception* to this observation is if you are a guru, mentor, coach, consultant, lawyer, doctor, professor, or career advisor.

21. They can put everyone at ease.

Do you know of someone in your family or circle of friends whom you feel *incredibly* comfortable around? Who are these people who can put everyone at ease?

Observe these people carefully. They accept others for who they are, letting go of the desire to change them. They don't seek unnecessary approval or recognition, or offer unsolicited advice. They enjoy querying and listening, which makes them interesting conversationalists. They aren't quick to judge people, and are largely solution seekers. Such people are approachable, self-assured, open-minded, secure, appreciative, and optimistic.

22. When a family member unexpectedly walks into the living room.

If you are visiting the home of a friend or colleague, observe what happens when an unexpected family member walks in. If the other person or people cringe, become quiet, start to get uncomfortable or uptight, then the newcomer has an overbearing or imperious attitude.

If the other family members smile or laugh, continuing the banter as they did before the person walked into the room, that means they are comfortable and relaxed around that person. Such people make others feel good about themselves. Are you that person?

23. The comfort level around the elderly.

Observe the comfort level of younger members of a family in the presence of the seniors of the family. If the younger members are extremely formal, reticent, or self-conscious, or if it seems they have bottled up their feelings, know that there is an emotional distance between them and their elders, a polite conformity in the relationship.

If the young are able to speak their minds and appear informal or casual (yet respectful), that is a sign they have reached a super-comfort level.

The exception to this observation is the practice within certain cultures, in which the young are expected to behave with great deference, showing respect to their elders.

24. Sudden Silence.

Sudden silence can say a lot. If you observe someone fall into a sudden silent mode, know that someone has said or done something that has upset them, possibly triggering anger, anxiety, stress, or resentment, or activating an emotional or painful memory.

If this happens to you and the person gives you the silent treatment for an extended period, know that it is designed to make you feel sorry or guilty, as if they want you to understand what is it like to feel what they're feeling.

And then there are people who go silent to exert control on you. In their silence, they want you to feel ignored, unwanted, or unworthy. They want to let you know you no longer exist for them, or they don't care about you, so that you beg them to talk to you again.

Some people go silent when they slip into a creative, reflective, or contemplative mindset, or when they're trying to find a solution to a problem. Such people cannot help but lapse into silence.

8

THE SUBTLE STINGINESS

25. They are emotionally stingy.

People aren't just money stingy, they are also *gratitude, apology, appreciation, compliment,* and *affection* stingy.

Observe how people thank, apologize, appreciate, compliment, or express affection. If they do so in merely one or two words—"Thank you," "Sorry," "Good job," "Well done," "Congratulations," "Appreciate it," or "Happy Birthday," they are emotionally stingy. This depicts the insecurity prevalent in their hearts or heads that dissuades them from saying a few more words or *wholeheartedly* expressing their gratitude, apology, appreciation, and so forth.

More often than not, such people hide behind age-old excuses—that they are a person of few words, or that they are informal with their loved ones—so their expression of celebration, gratitude, respect, praise, or regret is concise. However, in most instances such people prefer that the gratitude, apology, compliments, appreciation, and affection that come their way is poured out profusely and abundantly; or at the very least, is expressed in a sentence or two, not a word or two.

Why then are they so frugal in conveying their gratefulness, repentance, praise, or good wishes?

Making someone else feel bigger, happier, or more important than they, and doing so with hearty approbation, makes them feel small, less important, and insecure. It also reflects a lack of change, or a belief that they are inadequate. Thus, they continue to convey their feelings in one or two words.

26. Are they really generous?

Observe if a person is generous with his or her money, or generous with their spouse's money, or inherited money, or gift money. If a person is benevolent with money they did not earn, that may not mean the person is generous or giving. It is easy to be bighearted with family money or someone else's money. The real test of generosity is if they can be generous with their own funds or earned money.

27. They are affluent yet miserly when it comes to spending on others.

Observe the rich and prosperous who are liberal while spending money on *themselves*, and also enjoy being *generous* with other people's money and accepting their unbridled hospitality; but when it comes to reciprocation or spending money on others, they are largely close-fisted or miserly. Such a self-centered approach to wealth ignores the important karmic principle of money, which dictates that if a person wishes to prosper or flourish, he or she needs to keep money in circulation by sharing it with others in a sensible manner. This keeps the stream of money flowing, alive and vibrant. But if money is used only for personal pleasure, and not for the benefit of others, then money finds a way to desert such people.

Know that these people wouldn't really enjoy the material pleasures for long periods of time, as their money is then used to pay for colossal medical expenses, or alternatively, gets depleted because of unintended financial repercussions, or ends up with their inheritors sooner than envisaged.

9

THE TESTS OF CHARACTER

28. How do they deal with failure, rejection, or defeat.

Failure, rejection, and defeat reveal a lot about people. During such times, if a person continually flips out, makes excuses, beats himself up, plays the blame game, spreads lies about the person who rejected them, inflicts physical or emotional abuse on their partner or children, takes offense at any suggestion to do things differently or to bounce back with renewed vigor, then you know that person is experiencing social pain and humiliation. This pain, though, is really another name for their ego. Their fear, pessimism, aggression, and self-derogatory beliefs are on view, because they thought they were *never* going to fail, and failure means loss of control and respect.

While it may be natural that failure and rejection sting, causing pangs of regret or remorse, if the aggrieved person doesn't understand that failure, loss, and rejection are imperative for success, it is a sign they will lack the inner resilience to get back up after failure and rejection.

29. This family member or friend helped you financially and didn't let anyone know about it.

Know that if you ever received financial assistance from someone who didn't mention it to any other person, or did so without any need for reciprocation or to enhance their reputation, or to exert any indirect or direct power over you, to control or influence you, such a person is *rare*, compassionate, helpful, and considerate.

They know that the best form of help is done quietly, silently, or anonymously. They don't take any credit for their financial support or seek one iota of publicity from it, because they want to maintain your self-respect and dignity, and not make you feel small and insignificant in front of others. Such people extend help because they get happiness and satisfaction from doing so, and know what it feels like to take financial help from others out of compulsion or helplessness.

30. They treat people with lower economic status differently.

If you want to get to know someone's character, observe the following.

How do they treat:

a. The underprivileged, or people lower than their socio-economic status?

b. The doorman, cleaning lady, plumber, or electrician; the sanitation, retail, and fast food workers; the driver and the chauffeur; the customer service representative; and other service providers?

c. The restaurant server?

d. Their household staff?

Are they polite and courteous? Do they say "Please" and "Thank you"? Are they rude and abrupt, as if they were ordering the other person around? Do they skip the tip if their food is delayed by a few minutes? Do they sound dismissive or adopt a condescending tone?

If they have a patronizing attitude or exhibit an abrasive behavior, that's a huge red flag for you right there. Such people are power-trippers, insensitive, and inconsiderate, and act with a sense of entitlement. If they cannot treat people as equals, it is a sign they may also be disrespectful to you, some day in the near future.

31. Adversity or crisis reveals true character.

Observe a person in times of adversity, when their true character is revealed. If a person becomes an inveterate complainer, an incessant liar, succumbs to selfishness and greed, exploits the situation, cuts the salary of employees or lays them off *despite having the means or the resources to support them*, or fails to see any positives, their once-masked negative attitude and self-destructive mindset has come to the fore.

On the contrary, if a person turns adversity into an opportunity; develops a solution-oriented mindset; learns a new skill or hones existing talents; finds deeper meaning and purpose; extends a helping hand to a stranger, neighbor, peer, colleague, friend, or family member; and focuses on the positives, that person's strength of character, generous spirit, adaptability, optimism, and tenacity are unveiled. Remember, nothing highlights the true character of a person like adversity.

10

THE EYES AND FEET COMMUNICATE

32. Eyes are the window to your soul.

Study a person's eyes and you will be able to read their mind. "The eyes are the mirror of the soul and reflect everything that seems to be hidden; and like a mirror, they also reflect the person looking into them" (Paulo Coelho, *Manuscript Found in Accra*).

Exception: For those cultures where eye contact is considered rude or disrespectful, the observations appended below are not relevant.

a. The amount of eye contact a person makes with you during a conversation will reveal what he or she is thinking and feeling. If a person makes eye contact with you for 50–70 percent of the time, then he or she is confident, paying attention, and interested in what you are saying. If a person makes eye contact with you for 75–100 percent of the time, then he or she is either interested in you, attracted to you, or may have some ulterior motive behind the gaze (for instance, a creepy stare). If a person makes eye contact with you for 30–50 percent of the time or less, then he or she is either shy and introverted, nervous, preoccupied with some other thought, indifferent, or uninterested in what you are saying.

b. If a person doesn't make any eye contact with you or looks away when you speak, it denotes that nothing you've said has really registered in their mind. Alternatively, this may also mean that they are concealing something from you, lying to you, bored, or overly conscious of their surroundings.

c. During an interview, date, social rendezvous, or business meeting, if a person is looking down at the floor, the individual is feeling intimidated, nervous, or anxious.

d. If a person's eyes repeatedly move from side to side (assuming it isn't an eye defect or disorder) while talking or listening, it indicates that person is self-conscious, crafty, ambitious, and calculating.

33. The feet communicate.

Observe someone's feet, and it will tell you more about their intent.

a. In a conversation, a person's feet will point in the direction of the individual they are paying attention to, interested in, agree with, or are most comfortable around.

b. In a one-on-one discussion, if they pull their feet back or point them away from you, that is a sign of disagreement, disinterest, or discomfort. If their feet are pointed at the door or the exit, it means the person wants to leave.

c. If a person's feet are placed closely together, that is a sign of insecurity, shyness, or nervousness.

11

THE MOST IMPORTANT THINGS IN LIFE

34. What is the most important thing in life?

Ask people this question: "What is the most important thing in life—*time, education, wisdom, or money*?" If they say *time*, they are wise or far-sighted; if they say *education*, they value learning and knowledge; if they say *wisdom*, they are seekers of supreme or eternal truth; and if they say *money*, they are deeply pragmatic.

35. Their life purpose.

If you really want to get to know someone *quickly*, ask him or her this question: "What is your purpose in life?"

For those who opine that the purpose of life is *primarily* the incessant pursuit of pleasure, the quest for material objects (abundant money, lavish home, expensive cars, extravagant vacations), and a compulsive search for fame or power, you will find a big void in their life, an emptiness or a yearning that needs to be filled but that they pack with substitutes, like an epicurean life, or the comfort of pride and grandeur. Such people are outwardly focused, materialistic, and all about appearances (the labels and exclusive brands).

On the other hand, people with a purpose or who want to make a difference, who have a vision or who pursue their passion (discovered or cultivated), are positively optimistic, interesting, inspiring, experience driven, and usually inward looking. Know that they can manage an adversity or crisis better than people who feel their life lacks purpose, meaning, or direction.

36. As they get wiser, they become more selective.

As a person becomes wiser, he or she become more selective. Such people enjoy their own company the most, and the select few they consider members of their inner coterie. They don't rely on or require a lot of people to give them happiness, peace, comfort, and love. They rely on quality (not quantity) of relationships for their growth and well-being, and do not prescribe to the general notion that the more friends you have, the happier you are.

Being selective is not being selfish. Being selective enables them to have a more beautiful and significant existence. So, next time you meet a person who is selective in social relationships, know that they have a solid and intimate circle of friends that provides them the opportunity to stay invested in happiness, self-knowledge, and wisdom.

37. The self-induced learner, the competitive player, or the nurturer.

People who like to read books and listen to podcasts; go to museums; attend talks and lectures; watch dance, opera, plays, musicals, or *discerning* international films are intellectually curious and self-induced toward learning and development.

People who like to play sports or games (board, video, online, or card games), indulge in extensive travel, or are involved in politics are usually adventurous and competitive. People who are fond of babies, care for the elderly, as well as animals, are usually nurturing and sensitive souls.

38. They change with the times.

a. If they support the decision by their children, siblings, spouse or partner to follow an unconventional or unknown education or career path.

b. If they support their children's or sibling's

marriage to a person of a different religion or ethnicity.

c. If they support their LGBT children or siblings.

d. If they accept or support the decision by their children, siblings, spouse or partner to follow a different spiritual path than their own.

e. If they stay in the mode of continual learning and adaptability, and branch out of the comfort zone time and again.

39. So you think they are broad-minded?

The person who *willingly* accepts, appreciates, or encourages the inexperienced, the unknown, the small, the emerging, and the unconventional, or the individual who is *ahead* of their times, is truly the broad-minded, tolerant, and progressive. When you meet someone who embodies most of these attributes, know that you have then met an open-minded person. Analyze people against these parameters and you will know if they're truly broad-minded.

40. The books they read.

Observe a person's bookshelf or find out the type of books he or she reads, owns, borrows, or likes to discuss. It will tell you more about his or her personality, interests, and character.

If you're fond of nonfiction books, you have a proclivity for personal growth and development, or for enhancing your expertise on certain subjects. If you like reading classics or poetry, you are aesthetic, empathetic, observant, insatiably curious, and prefer knowing people deeply. If you enjoy historical fiction, you have an eye for detail and a tendency of being a perfectionist. If you are into horror, in all likelihood you have a bit of a dark side, even though you are, for the most part, a peaceful person. If you love fantasy novels, chances are you're a dreamer and a creative thinker with a wild imagination. If you prefer romance novels, odds are you're a romantic yourself. If you *primarily* read bestsellers, you're focused on trends and what's currently "in" at the moment. And if you love thrillers or suspense, then you're curious, adventurous, and imaginative.

41. They enjoy their own company and don't get bored.

A person who enjoys his own company and doesn't get bored is an interesting and empowered person, as long as you know how to get him or her to talk—and then you listen for most of the conversation. *If a person can be alone and yet not feel lonely, or be with many and yet feel alone (not lonely),* then such a person is an engaging conversationalist. It is up to you to draw that person into a riveting discussion by conversing on topics that interest him or her.

Remember the brutal truth-*only boring people get bored, because they need external stimulation or activities so as not to feel bored.* Those who have a purpose, a passion, a hobby, or diverse interests, or who walk the path of self-discovery, *rarely* get bored.

42. Quiet people notice things that others overlook.

Observe quiet people, for they have a fascinating inner journey for you to explore. They are incredibly observant and notice the things that others overlook. That makes them great judges of character and difficult to fool. They think carefully before they say anything.

The quiet one has a rich, inner life and prefers to fly under the radar, and this makes them insightful and creative. They can enrich your life by the power of the ideas and solutions they bring to your world. Because most of them are good listeners, value learning, and enjoy stimulating conversations, they turn out to be interesting people. You will see their eyes light up when certain topics are mentioned, and if you guide the conversation in that direction, you will realize how smart they are.

43. Receiving constructive criticism.

Observe how people handle constructive criticism when it comes from a sagacious well-wisher or a mentor who is aware of their needs, circumstances, strengths, flaws, and intentions. If they accept it with poise and openness and are willing to act on the feedback, that means they are receptive to listening, change, and growth. If not, they will offer explanations or excuses, or get defensive or angry.

Keep in mind that a lot depends on how the constructive criticism is delivered or expressed, and when. If the timing is inappropriate or the tone was abrasive or harsh, then even though the critique might make sense, chances are it won't be accepted.

44. They hire people brighter or smarter than they.

If you want to know how *smart* a leader or entrepreneur is, observe who they hire. The smartest leaders and entrepreneurs hire people who are better, brighter, or more talented than they, because they are *truly* self-confident, capable, adaptable, and farsighted.

45. They share their success or expertise mantras *before* they retire.

People who share their success or expertise mantras *in the prime of their careers* with anyone who is willing to benefit or profit from them are transparent and secure, with a generous or abundant mindset.

12

UNEARTH THE UNHEALTHY EGO

46. Accept a compliment with class or conceit.

When you appreciate or compliment someone, observe how he or she accepts the compliment. If they return it or pass the credit on to their mentor, to someone equivalent to their rank or status, to the Almighty, or to luck, know that such people are usually humble or down-to-earth. If they pass it along to a direct report, or someone lower in rank or status, they are big-hearted and admirably classy. If they acknowledge the appreciation and immediately self-promote, directly or indirectly, they are self-conceited or a braggart.

47. Where social status matters most.

Observe people who ask questions about your income, whether you own your home or not and what kind of neighborhood it's in, if you fly business class or economy, and other indicators of net worth that they can use as points of comparison. Such people consider social status the most important determination of self-worth.

Know that if you are of *far* superior social status than what may be attainable for another person, they may feel envious but may also use your privileged rank to heighten their stature among friends and family members. A classic example is name-dropping to impress others. However, if you belong to the same social class, a person may pretend to be your friend but still be secretly envious of you, and may not be able to take joy at your or your family's success. They may play it down or dismiss it, pretend it's no big deal.

Remember, they are competing with you, even if you're not competing with them. They will continually feel the need to be one step ahead of you. They may undermine you in different ways, sometimes on the pretext of being funny, sometimes by commenting on your beliefs or appearance, and sometimes by planting self-doubt. Their intention is to influence others to see you in a poor light. Know that they are insecure, have low self-esteem, and want to be in control.

Recognize the status conscious by how they reduce

almost everything to material considerations. When they intently observe or repeatedly comment on the stylish clothes you wear or the car you drive, their focus is on the money these things must have cost.

For people whose primary focus is the pursuit of social status, and who lack any other purpose or calling in life, you will notice that as they get older, they begin to feel restless, empty, and bored.

48. They like to name-drop.

People who continually name-drop to show how well connected they are do so to impress others, to appear important and special. Name-droppers are attention-seekers, and they wish to elevate their public persona by connecting with the better-known, wealthier, or more powerful. They are ambitious, egotistical (overinflated sense of self), and exhibitionists.

49. They like to say "I know."

When you hear someone repeatedly say "I know" (the know-it-all), it implies false pride or arrogance. Such a person does not want to appear inferior or admit his or her ignorance about the topic being discussed. It also delineates a resistance to learning and change.

The other instance when people frequently say "I know" is when they aren't comfortable with (they may be upset too) or interested in what's being discussed, and wish to change the subject or end the conversation.

50. The person will become boring over time.

An individual who *doesn't:*

a. enjoy his or her own company. If you *can't* spend time alone and *enjoy* being by yourself, you will struggle to become an interesting person;

b. read books;

c. listen to meaningful podcasts;

d. watch engaging, interesting, or inspirational videos;

e. ask the right questions and search for answers (they won't develop an inquisitive mind);

f. discover or chase a purpose, make time for his or her passion, pursue a skill or a hobby, focus on his or her interests, *or*

g. see any value in the lifetime pursuit of learning, knowledge, or wisdom… such a person will become *boring* over time.

51. They constantly criticize or nitpick.

People who have formed a habit of nitpicking or criticizing others have usually been criticized in days gone by, or been a victim of fussy fault-finding in the past. Such people are essentially pessimistic, and they struggle to see the positive or the good in people around them. A subtle ego of "I know" intermixed with uncontrolled self-righteousness becomes their second nature. You can trace the roots of their critical nature right back to a hypercritical parent.

52. The "I" person.

If a person *doesn't:*

a. open and hold the door for others;

b. offer to share his or her umbrella (when it starts raining) with a coworker who might have forgotten theirs;

c. wait for people to get off the train before he or she boards the train;

d. consider the feelings of people who matter before making an important decision (not those that stop you from following your dreams, purpose, or passion), *or*

e. treat others the way they would want to be treated… know that you have run into an inconsiderate, discourteous, and selfish person.

53. Success came much later than expected.

Whenever you see a successful person brag about his or her achievements or material acquisitions, know that success came to that person later in life, after years or decades of struggle, drudgery, and perseverance. Such bragging is a sign of insecurity and a deliberate attempt to maneuver others to form a favorable opinion of them. These people fish for compliments and need constant approval.

54. Their golden words are *I*, *Me*, or *Mine*.

If a person uses the words *I*, *Me*, and *Mine* frequently, that is a sign of an individual who has an inflated sense of importance and abilities. Such people can be warm and generous, and yet also arrogant and self-centered. They may be outwardly impressive, but are inwardly fragile and thin-skinned, suffer from low self-esteem, which is why they try hard to get attention and spruce up their self-worth.

55. They suffer from professional envy.

Watch a person's reaction when he or she meets (or hears of) a friend, family member, or acquaintance in the same profession or business who is more successful, valued, or accomplished than he or she. If they are dismissive or critical of the successful person (if it isn't a matter of ethics or values), then it is a sign of envy, because comparison creates discontent.

56. They like to force their opinions or ideas on others.

Take note of the person who aggressively tries to prove a point, argues in an unsavory manner, or forces his or her opinions, perspectives, ideas, or beliefs onto others. Such individuals may have good intentions, but they demonstrate a domineering side of their personality that is a front for pure ego, some level of intolerance, and a desire to be heard and accepted.

57. They praise you for your ability or talent, and not your effort.

If people praise you for your natural ability, for what seems like an innate talent or skill, *and not* your hard work, that implies an air of deprecation, as though you were simply lucky to be born with an *inborn* talent or skill, and your determination and effort had nothing do with your success.

58. They are quick to judge others.

People who form an opinion about everything, judge too quickly, or make unfounded assumptions before considering all the facts have a distorted view of others, and tend to be narrow-minded, inherently negative and stubborn, and lack empathy. Often a judgmental parent has raised such a person.

59. They operate from fear.

If a person is operating from a position of extreme caution or continued ambivalence, and has *stopped* taking chances or stepping into the unknown, then know that fear and insecurity is holding them back and calling the shots in their life.

60. Know them in success and good luck, failure and bad luck.

Observe how people handle success, prosperity, good luck, and fame. Do they consider themselves entirely self-made? Do they take credit for their own success, or do they *truly* believe in the collective action and intelligence of their team members that made it happen? If their pride, ego, insecurity, or ignorance keeps them from recognizing the contributions of others, then it means they value self-glorification above all.

If they continuously give credit to the team or to the stakeholders who helped them get ahead in life, they are unassumingly modest, mindful, and respectful of their colleagues' contributions. Such people are thoughtful, empathetic, and generous by nature.

Watch how people cope with failures and bad luck. Do they take responsibility for their failures and short-comings? Have they learned valuable lessons? If not, they are doomed to repeat the same errors and are less likely to persevere, learn, and adapt. Such people suffer from the arrogance of ignorance.

13

EXCITING SMALL INSIGHTS

61. They use the word *BUT* often.

When you discuss an innovative or unconventional idea, option, or path that you wish to embark on, and someone uses the word *BUT* more than a few times, as if it is to oppose or dismiss the idea or option *outright*, it indicates that they like to play it safe and stay in their comfort zone. However, if the word *BUT* is said to discuss or challenge the new idea or option, because the person is considering it from different aspects or perspectives, then it implies thoughtful decision-making.

62. Offer them something *free* more than three times.

Offer a person something free more than three times, and if he or she accepts the offer each time you make it, that is good enough to know his or her character. Know that such people like to take advantage of the generosity of others. They are selfish and manipulative. They are takers. Takers like to take and givers like to give; and if takers know they can get away with taking (for free) and taking more without any reciprocity, they will try to make the most of it. Taking will then become a habit. Takers are self-focused and carry a sense of entitlement. However, there are exceptions when it is a family matter or a crisis, or if there's a cultural or affordability aspect associated with the free offerings or favors. In such circumstances, the taking is understandable, because it would be considered insulting or foolish to say no.

63. Observe our parents.

We are a product of our upbringing and parenting, including environment and circumstances. So if you want to know a person better, observe his or her parent(s) and their nature, character, personality, and persona. The positive or negative traits of a parent will not necessarily be passed on to their children, but there is a likelihood that at least a few of the positive qualities or disagreeable attributes will be inherited from the parent(s).

To know yourself better, you can analyze the parenting style of your mom and dad—controlling, disciplinarian, easy-going, nurturing, indulgent, hands-off, or neglectful. This will help you understand your temperament and how it compares to your parents'. You may be surprised that you are like your parents.

Normally (barring exceptions), behind every domineering personality is an overbearing and controlling parent who repressed his or her children's need for independence and freedom. These children grow up to become intolerant of any type of dissent.

64. They laugh the most.

People who laugh the most or the loudest are *either:*

a. carefree, kind-hearted, emotional, and generous, or

b. The loneliest or the unhappiest (they have gone through trying times), yet don't take life too seriously, and are sensitive enough not to unload their problems on others.

65. The best and the worst days of their life.

Ask a person to look back and share with you the best and the worst days of his or her life. This will tell you a lot about what a person treasures most, what troubles them, and how they overcame crises and challenges.

66. The unrevealed pause.

During a one-on-one conversation with someone, if you observe that they pause before they tell you something and then change the subject, then that is a sign that they were about to reveal a harsh truth or share a piece of uncomfortable, private, or important information, but then chose not to.

67. They love the words *Should, Must,* and *Right.*

People who love to use the words *Should, Must,* and *Right* like to set high standards, live by the rules, and take initiative at work and in life.

68. The choice of words says a lot about a person.

Watch the words people say *often* or the words they use most *commonly*. Choice of words determines their mindset. If they use words that encourage, uplift, and energize others, or express gratitude regardless of their circumstances, then such people are *truly* positive. However, if their most-used words are largely discouraging, cynical, and belittling, or reek of self-doubt, resentment, or a victim mentality, then such people are *truly* negative. Pay attention to how often they use the words *yes* and *no*. The more a person uses the word *yes* or affirmative expressions, the more positive they are.

69. The happier couple.

Couples or partners that subtly, candidly, or fondly compliment or promote each other in front of family members and friends are usually in a happier space than those who don't show their appreciation for each other in public.

70. The complete opposites as couples, yet happy together (not because of compatibility).

Observe spouses or couples who are *complete or polar opposites* and yet live happily together. They are able to do so primarily because they are devoid of financial stress, have ditched or released their emotional baggage, or given each other a free rein.

71. The truth after a few drinks.

When a person is drunk, what he or she says to you then is the truth, the hard, the bitter, the embarrassing, or the sweet truth. When high on alcohol, the mask comes off and you will witness another person's true self. Observe people after a few drinks, and you will see them for who they really are.

72. They live in the past.

Notice people who are stuck in the past, continually comparing it to the present and hoping the present can somehow resemble the past; or alternatively, they cannot stop recounting *past* hurts, regrets, or disappointments. Life and its circumstances, tragedies, or hardships have taken a toll on such people. They may have gotten this trait from their parents, who in their time were constantly mourning the past.

73. The sales professional who is pressuring you.

The sales professional who is pressuring, pestering, or forcing you for a purchase is either struggling to meet his sales targets or making an *unusually* high sales commission.

74. Observe the extrovert and the introvert.

Extroverts need constant contact, so they like being around people and love meeting new people. It energizes them. They love to talk (they are great at striking up conversations with strangers) and enjoy being the center of attention. To the extrovert, the external world provide them the stimuli to feel alive and appreciated. They look to outside sources for ideas and inspiration. If you find a person struggling to spend time alone, chances are he or she is an extrovert.

Notice people who are more inward focused and in tune with their internal thoughts and feelings. They tend to be reserved and introspective, and are more likely to think before they speak. They enjoy spending time alone or tend to prefer the company of close friends. Instead of having a large social circle, they form a few intimate and profound relationships.

If you see someone who, after an extended day of work or social activity, retreats in solitude to read a book, enjoy a peaceful walk, listen to music, or indulge in writing, sketching, painting, or any other artistic or creative hobby as a way to relax and recharge, chances are he or she is an introvert.

75. What pain points are they uncomfortable discussing?

Observe people's faces or expressions when you say something they're uncomfortable discussing, or when they say something that brings back painful memories. It could be an estranged relationship, physical or psychological abuse, extreme discrimination, a financial setback, a business failure, an agonizing decision, or a destroyed career. You will then know their pain points.

Listen to what people don't say or discuss. For example, if a person doesn't talk about an estranged friend or family member, then he or she is living with a conflict or angst they are reluctant to reveal, perhaps too ashamed or embarrassed to do so; or they have moved on and just don't care about the other person anymore. Also, if they avoid a topic or subtly divert the conversation, that indicates they aren't comfortable discussing the matter with you.

76. They don't flaunt their wealth or material possessions.

People who don't talk about wealth or flaunt their material acquisitions are people with *old money*, those who have been wealthy for many generations. Even if someone notices or points out the amassed wealth, they stay grounded and prefer discussing the higher purpose that is behind the generational fortunes. The exception in this scenario are those *new rich* (the nouveau riche or the new moneyed) who do not display the wealth they have created and don't resort to conspicuous consumption, because they like to stay under the radar of the prying income tax officials, pesky fundraisers, or those that might come knocking on their doors to borrow money from them.

77. They are trustworthy.

Lend a person a book or some money, or let them borrow your clothes or power tools, anything you are comfortable in lending. If the person repays the money or returns the borrowed book, clothes, or tools, *and does so without you asking for it,* then the person is trustworthy. If not, he or she is untrustworthy. The exception here is the person who has the *intention* of repaying but cannot afford to do so, or is unable to because of unforeseen circumstances.

78. The prism of simplicity.

People who *claim* to be simple because they find happiness in small things but live in *big* homes or mansions, or lavish condominiums or apartments, who drive expensive cars and have a retinue of domestic staff, travel business or first class, wear fashionable clothes and buy expensive gadgets, aren't really simple. They may be simpler than the superrich, but they aren't simple people. They are pretending to be simple, living through the convenient prism of simplicity.

They have a choice, and by living it large, expensive, trendy, or lavish, they indicate that they enjoy social status, reputation, power, privacy, or exclusivity, even if they help the underprivileged, lead nonprofit organizations, run charities, or give money to support good causes.

79. Why don't more parents create the extraordinary or the exceptional?

Observe extraordinary people and ascertain if they went from being ordinary to extraordinary because of their parents.

Take note of the fact that most parents teach their children *only* what they know, what they believe in, and what they have experienced. They don't expose them to what they don't know, don't believe in, or haven't experienced.

This reasoning may create rich and successful children, but barring exceptions, it won't make a child extraordinary unless the child is a born genius or works hard to do something *out of the ordinary*.

80. When they invite you over for negotiations.

When you enter negotiations or decisive meetings, the person who invited you to his territory, home, or workplace, the location of his choice, knows that he or she has an advantage of winning the negotiations, or can at least steer it toward his or her advantage. This is because when they are on their home turf or a familiar area and can get you to come to them, they become the one controlling the situation. And the one who has control has power. They know that *you*, the invited person, is in unfamiliar territory, where you are likely to be more polite, giving, compromising, nervous, or anxious, or might rush into an agreement you may later regret.

81. They have no permanent friends or enemies.

Observe people who have no permanent friends or enemies and are looking for power or prosperity. Such people are political opportunists or moneyed opportunists. They belong only to those who can help them advance their cause. They have no fixed beliefs or principles, and maneuverability and adaptability is their greatest strength.

There is another type of opportunist: wisdom personified, or the detached spiritualist. They don't form deep associations or attachments with anyone because they understand the impermanent and transitory nature of life, and they practice the subtle art of detachment in all relationships.

82. Our choices reflect who we are.

Our destiny, progress, and happiness is determined by our choices, and you can get to know people better by observing the choices they make or have made—marital, education, and career; parenting and friends; material acquisitions (luxury versus nonluxury) and saving and investment decisions; diet, exercise, and fitness choices; and other interests, namely, volunteering, self-development, travel, creative or artistic endeavors. The results and consequences of their choices will help you really know someone.

83. Intuition or evidence—who follows what.

Most scientists, medical doctors, engineers, mathematicians, finance czars, and emerging technologies professionals (the Internet of Things, Artificial

Intelligence, machine learning, blockchain, robotics, virtual reality, augmented reality, mixed reality, biometrics, and more) base their important decisions on data, facts, statistics, studies, evidence, logical reasoning, numbers, or algorithms.

Most political, creative, spiritual, artistic, and visionary leaders, innovators (business, the arts, and beyond), sales, marketing, and communications professionals base their critical decisions on intuition, gut feeling, or a hunch.

84. Most people don't change.

Observe your family members and friends carefully. Have they changed over the years, or are they more the way they always were?

While there are exceptions, most people don't change, because change requires recognizing their character traits that could do with a marked improvement. This explains why most people have a solution for other people's problems but not their own. There is a tendency to explain one's shortcomings and failures by blaming someone else.

Look around you and observe the people you know. The cousin who was stingy as a teenager continues to be a penny-pincher *thirty years later*; the mother who reveled in gossip twenty years ago continues to tittle-tattle; the aunt who was deeply critical while you were growing up carries on with judging people harshly; the father who imposed a career choice on his children upon college graduation continues to interfere in their adult lives; the sister who in high school was as cool as a cucumber displays the same calm before bungee jumping, *ten years later*; the short-tempered brother who snapped at trivial things in the early phase of his career now loses his temper at his team members; the fifteen-year-old niece who raised money for the homeless started a non-profit for poverty alleviation *twenty-five years later*; the friend who demonstrated tremendous flexibility at the workplace that took him places now exhibits incredible adaptability in a cross-border marriage.

People change, so we believe, because we mistake human migration, expertise, travel, refinement, erudition, elegance, and charm as indicators of real change. They can be, but only for those who wish to change of their own volition by becoming aware of the mistakes they keep repeating, of the important areas of their lives where they haven't willingly changed. This impels them to take corrective action to embrace change.

14

THE POWER GAMES PEOPLE PLAY

85. They're way too charming.

People who are too quick to charm—they always say the right thing, appear to be the perfect person, engage you in riveting conversation, and flatter or sway you with their sweet words—know that these are means of disarming you. For beneath all the beguiling charm is a self-absorbed, cunning, and manipulative person.

Be cautioned, these intoxicating charmers are masters at hiding things, skeletons in their closet they don't want you to find.

86. They habitually talk over others.

People who frequently talk over others or keep cutting them off midsentence were talked over too at some point in their lives. These interrupters are quick thinkers, perceptive and intelligent, yet impatient and insecure, more likely to use power plays to their advantage.

87. They deliberately contradict or oppose you.

People who *intentionally* contradict or oppose you to irritate you or stir you up, so that you lose control over your emotions and thoughts and disclose critical secrets are calculating and hypercompetitive.

88. They play the game of one-upmanship.

If a person is always trying to one-up you in a conversation and claims that his or her education, status, material possessions, reputation, or lineage (or the achievements of his or her family members and friends) is superior to yours, that person is subtly ignoring or belittling your or your family's accomplishments, and is delineating how he or she is more important than you. Such behavior indicates that the one-upper has a fragile self-esteem induced by an insecure and pompous mindset.

89. They indulge in *excessive* praise.

When a person praises you *excessively* (your popularity, looks, achievements, intelligence, creativity, or personality) and that praise sounds insincere or appears calculated, you should know that the person is trying to wrangle something out of you.

When a person goes a step beyond sheer flattery to talk primarily about topics that are of interest to you (that may or may not interest them) *only* to get your attention or make you happy, he or she is craftily maneuvering you. They may be buying peace, seeking your approval, or want some favor or assistance from you. Alternatively, if they are embarrassingly fulsome in their appreciation, it is a sign they want to gain entry into your inner circle. Also, as you get to know them, you start confiding your darkest secrets or reveal your most personal information, which this person can use against you for their own benefit. Such people, who use disingenuous praise to pursue their agendas, are at the core manipulative and exploitative.

90. The financially insensitive.

During a global crisis or pandemic, when millions of people have been laid off, or furloughed from their jobs, or forced to take pay cuts, and the world is afflicted with unemployment, financial uncertainty, separation, anguish, death, and grief, observe people who have made smart financial decisions but *show no compassion.* They brag about their investments or other symbols of wealth *around people who are struggling financially or figuring out ways to keep their families fed.* Such people are insensitive, arrogant, and unkind.

91. The patriarch or the matriarch dominate the joint family or family-owned business for an *extended* period of time.

In a joint family (immediate and extended family living under the same roof) or an established family-owned business, if the patriarch or the matriarch *cannot* hand over the baton to the next generation at the right time, or can't stop from intruding into the young members' decision-making process even after becoming a senior citizen, then know that such a patriarch or matriarch is a self-seeking individual who can't let go of power, control, or authority, even upon attaining the *new retirement age (age 70)*.

92. They make an ostentatious display of wealth or power, or clamor about depleted resources.

When a person shows off their wealth, power, and accomplishments, or alternatively, is clamorous about his or her depleted resources or bankrupt state, go beyond such deception or guile, for the truth may be opposite of what is being presented to you.

93. They worm out your secrets; how about theirs?

People who have an uncanny ability to unearth secrets or sensitive information from you without *ever* sharing their secrets with you are astute, evasive, and guarded.

94. The game of authoritarian leaders and followers.

If an individual prefers to have sycophants around him or her who will follow orders or diktats with precision, then that person is an authoritarian; and the attendants or followers who rush to obey these orders to earn praise and rewards (money, status, power, or control) become admired disciples. In the game of autocratic leaders and their followers, there are hierarchies, and the climb to become the greatest or the best disciple is a way to eventually emerge as a new leader with ardent followers.

95. They knowingly say less than necessary.

People who knowingly say less than necessary, who offer short answers or terse solutions, are usually aware that they have more power, and more control over their emotions, than the person who talks more, has no filter, or is open and honest about his or her feelings.

They know that the longer they keep quiet or the

sooner they get others to talk (while they listen attentively), the more power they wield over others, based
on the insights and information they gather from the
person who talks freely. Such people are very perceptive, keen observers, enigmatic, and shrewd. Please
note that this observation doesn't apply to the wise and
the enlightened, or people who are naturally quiet or
reserved.

96. The favor that you were reminded of.

Family members, friends, peers, colleagues, or business
partners who do you a favor (small or big) and remind
you of it subtly, repeatedly, or in front of others *(done to
get importance and recognition)* are people who wish to
exert control or power over you. This is why they keep
a mental record book (or account) of any favor granted
to you.

By extending you a favor, they exert influence in an
indirect way. The favor wasn't a favor, but a mechanism
that they'll activate when it suits them. In essence, you
owe one back to them. However, the people who do
you a favor *silently* without ever talking about it, or who
brush it aside in an unassuming manner when reminded
by you, do you a favor *without* the need for recognition
or any desire to exert influence or control over you.

97. These people want power.

In many countries and governments, associations and organizations, power is concentrated in the hands of a few people. Observe that the people who seek power keep their eyes on the individuals who control the power or hold the cards. They try to get closer to the people in power or the power brokers, or congregate in deference around a powerful or strong personality, because they crave power; and they become willful followers of those who enjoy power, control, and authority.

The game of power has leaders and followers, and in time the followers become the power centers (or leaders) because of their need to retain power or acquire greater power. So the game and hierarchy of power-hungry leaders and followers continues.

98. They give lavish gifts.

People who like to give luxury or extraordinarily expensive gifts do so either to exert influence over the recipient or to nurture and buy their loyalty.

99. Your driving reveals your personality.

If a person likes to *always* drive the car, even when others would like to do so and can drive as well, that delineates a person who likes to be in control, which is effectively about power.

If a person drives like he or she owns the road with disregard for road etiquette and rules (turning without signaling, or veering into other lanes without checking their mirrors), then this is precisely how he or she will treat others in personal relationships. Such a person is selfish, disrespectful, inconsiderate, and irresponsible.

If the driver resorts to habitual swearing, obscene gestures, or aggressive driving, including frequent horn honking, it is a sign of an impatient, frustrated (or miserable), angry, and insecure person.

15

AUTHENTIC SPIRITUALITY VERSUS BUSINESS OF SPIRITUALITY

100. This is how you recognize an authentic spiritual guru.

To recognize a credible spiritual guru, discreetly observe their *acquired* material wealth (empire) and the aura of glamour that surrounds them. If their coffers are full of gifts and donations (or they charge a fee for their spiritual teaching or services), and marketing, merchandising, advertising, social media, and public-relations strategies are used to gain credulous followers, then that spirituality has turned into a business.

The quest to discover an authentic spiritual guru or enlightened master starts by finding answers to two important questions: Does the guru impart his or her teachings without recourse to publicity? Do they offer their sermons without any type of commercial commitment that is driven by gifts, charity, donations, or fees?

A spiritual guru (*guru* is a Sanskrit word that means dispeller of darkness) may be a reservoir of knowledge, and can justify acceptance of money or a fee for sharing that spiritual knowledge. That may be acceptable or absolutely fine, but do know that such a spiritual master can only give you knowledge—perhaps abundant knowledge—about spirituality, self-discovery, and self-realization. But being a fountain of knowledge is different from being a fountain of wisdom, for *the true* spiritual guru's teachings are *free*. They do not charge a fee for the wisdom they share.

If a person *makes a show* of being perfect, saintly, charitable, philanthropic, supremely tolerant, or progressive, it often is contrary to reality. The perfect spiritual exterior may disguise a penchant for power, dominance, and the limelight, or mask strong carnal desires. Ignore the front that people display and instead plumb the depths to figure out their true character.

Don't fall for the charm, charisma, or popularity of the spiritual guru you wish to follow. Observe and evaluate them before you become their devotee.

You will find genuine saints, spiritual gurus, and seekers who *don't* feel the need to publicize their spiritual instruction, learning, or wisdom, and who don't seek fame and power to attract or influence hundreds of thousands of followers. That then is the authentic spiritual guru who can lead a follower from darkness to light, and from ignorance to self-realization.

FINAL INSIGHTS

To find extraordinary happiness and success, *pursue your passion, work with your intuition, learn as a child, and adapt as water.*

Opposites attract, but compatibility preserves.

Great ideas are born out of debate and conflict.

Your secrets should be as safe as valuables in a locker.

Relationships are about bringing smiles to sullen faces.

Emotional outbursts and domination are signs of help-lessness and little self-control.

Meaningful relationships require compassionate communication and a high level of acceptance to thrive.

Material abundance devoid of love and trust can provide a house, but not a home, billions of dollars in wealth, but not even a thousand dollars of happiness.

Learn and play chess. It will teach you the virtues of patience and flexibility, and also enhance your powers of observation, and decision-making skills.

Even if you are right, no one ever wins an argument. Leave others to learn from their own experience and not your forced or throttled suggestions or perspectives.

All that glitters is not gold, and all that sparkles is not sold. Professional success without happiness and peace at home cannot provide enduring happiness.

Kids of famous or illustrious parents have to do things out of the ordinary or accomplish twice as much to carve their own identity.

Live as if today is your last day on this planet and remember to wear this on your sleeve each day. You will then become the best friend, the favorite supervisor, the unrivaled sweetheart, the wisest adviser, and the greatest listener.

An individual who prefers material possessions over relationships, and a person who can't stop caring or worrying about what others think about them, can never provide profound happiness to others.

Ask for help, even if you are smart or capable, and befriend people who are achievers, believers, and positive-minded strugglers, even if they have failed repeatedly. Stay away from the pessimistic, the disparager, and the skeptic.

Care, but do not brook interference. Share, but do not lose all you have. Respect, but do not become powerless. Love, but do not spoil. Listen, but do not become sub-servient. Empathize, but do not become overprotective.

A universal truth: *no matter how smart, spiritual, influential, or successful you may be, there is always that one person in your life who cannot be convinced, persuaded, or won over.*

Avoid prolonged argument with a pompous or overbearing family member or friend, and probing individuals who claim to be all-knowing. Time spent with such people will inhibit personal growth and development.

True eminence is not just about reaching the zenith of fame or wealth. It is about rediscovery, relearning, and reinvention. It is about the master always staying a student. It is the point where the end and the beginning tango.

The journey from good to great lies in destroying what you zealously created by surpassing your previous creation time and again, and yet retaining the disposition of a novice.

Triumphs are short-lived in the twenty-first century. The speed of change is so rapid that you cannot bask in the glory of your accomplishments. Yesterday ended last night and today is a new day. Keep learning, keep adapting, and stay humble.

Famous or celebrated people have two disparate realities of life, one pleasant–*a person whose time has come*, the other, a harsh truth–*a person whose time has ceased.* Nothing lasts forever.

The art of engaging conversation is to show genuine interest in others, encourage others to open up, ask interesting or insightful questions to deepen the level of conversation, practice active listening, and to speak as little as possible about yourself.

Novelty is for the extraordinary. Share your unconventional or original ideas only with those people who are open-minded, optimistic, risk-takers, or who can stomach an idea whose time has yet to come. Most people live within their comfort zones and cannot digest rarity.

Your expertise can desert you when required most. Mother Nature abominates ego of any kind. There comes a point in life where excellence and achievements of the past abandons us in the present, we muck up today, our advice or initiatives go haywire, and Nature being a great leveler mows down the seeds of our pride.

The best ideas come from the most unexpected individual. Explore and absorb ideas for new products and services that come from your kids or young children. High school or college dropouts, illiterate and functional illiterates are also a great source to tap for unmatched or unheard ideas.

The contest between an accomplished *secure* individual and a successful *arrogant* person exists only in the mind of the latter. For the egotistical, defeat is unacceptable, and external victories are a way of feeling secure. For the accomplished *secure*, it does not matter because all battles are waged within the self and not outside.

Observe animals closely. They teach us valuable leadership and business lessons. Learn teamwork and collaboration from an ant, strategy from a fox, espionage from a cat, vigilance from a dog, and the capacity to assimilate and store (knowledge) from a camel.

The best relationships are marred not because of the actual words used, but because the tone was harsh or rude. Some excellent suggestions or ideas are not accepted merely because of the tone in which they were conveyed. The impolite tongue used as a sarcastic weapon creates a permanent wound, whereas the genteel voice as a positive force reaches the heart and the soul of the listener.

A happy relationship means working on adopting the same interests, condoning faults, accepting quirks or a different temperament, providing room to experiment, space to evolve, and more importantly, honing the ability to have long conversations. With age, conversation skills become as imperative as any other aspect of a fulfilling relationship.

There is a difference between aggressive and effective action. Aggression may lead to success in the short-term, but it is reacting forcefully to a competitor's move. That means you lose control and play into the hands of your competitor. Assertive and effective action is to stay composed and frustrate competitors by making them react to your moves. Focus on winning the marathon and not the 100-meter dash.

Two minds are not the same. If the population of a country is 350 million, it means there are 350 million minds with beliefs or habits that differ from each other. If one of Mother Nature's elements–*fire*–cannot change and become *water*, then it is futile to expect an individual to change to your way of thinking, until the person does so out of his or her own volition.

Befriend those who have an opinion yet are not judgmental; who are rich, famous, or successful and yet modest; who have little but have not stopped chasing their dreams; who have experienced pain and yet can laugh at themselves; who stand by you in good and bad times; who can motivate when all seems lost; who have lost much and yet have the courage to bounce back; who are continually learning and changing; and who live life to the fullest, even as they honor the responsibilities that come with it.

From the *game of tennis* learn the "Rule of 100" to reduce or defuse relationship friction by staying calm, and saying the right thing at the right time.

When you're playing tennis and wish to return a powerful serve that is coming your way at 80 miles per hour, don't hit the ball back at 80 miles per hour, for you will not only lose the point, but will also mistime the ball. Instead, return the powerful serve with a well-timed 20 miles per hour shot. You add 80 miles per hour with 20 miles per hour; you get 100 miles per hour. Remember the *Rule of 100.* If the opponent serves the tennis ball at 50 miles per hour, you return the ball to him at 50 miles per hour. You add 50 miles per hour with 50 miles per hour; you get 100 miles per hour.

If you apply the *Rule of 100* to all types of relationships, you will find happiness and success. *Good timing is everything. If you can get your timing right, you can afford to get a lot of other things wrong.*

Karma where science and spirituality converge, and where the ancient and the modern meet is not just about cause and effect, action and reaction, or sowing and reaping, it is also about strengthening relationships, or destroying relationships and careers. Our beliefs, habits, words, actions, and thoughts constitute "Good Karma and Bad Karma" or "Positive Karma and Negative Karma."

The karma currency grows every moment, every day in our karmic bank account regardless of the effects of our good or bad deeds.

We can either do something positive, meaningful, inspiring, or honorable and build our good karma bank account, or we can give, share, care, appreciate, or express gratitude and grow our positive karma bank account. Alternatively, we can hurt or ruin relationships and careers with toxic words, anger, greed, lust, or ego to build our bad karma bank account, or we can gossip, backbite, or pass judgment to grow our negative karma bank account. In essence, whatever we put out into the universe is exactly what we will receive or attract back from it.

The choice is ours. We have the freedom to choose our beliefs, habits, words, actions, and thoughts, but we *do not* have the freedom to choose its outcome, result, or consequences. Choose wisely. Remember *"For every action, there is an equal and opposite reaction. As you sow, so shall you reap. If you plant the thorny acacia tree (babul tree) how can you reap mangoes?"*

ABOUT THE AUTHOR

PUSHPENDRA MEHTA is the author of the novel *The Suitable Inheritor* and the nonfiction books *Win the Battles of Life & Relationships* and *Tomorrow's Young Achievers,* which have earned him an internationally loyal readership.

For many years, he has been a student of human emotions and behavior, influenced by Sir Arthur Conan Doyle's fascinating fictional detective character, Sherlock Holmes. This has enabled him to draw discerning conclusions from the smallest of observations, and to hone his skills as a writer, storyteller, marketer, and mentor.

He considers his exposure to disparate people, places, and situations his biggest asset. Interaction with the privileged and the underprivileged, both in the East and the West, has enriched his understanding of the game of life and relationships. Pushpendra was raised in India and now lives in Atlanta. He is an alumnus of Northwestern University and Sydenham College of Commerce & Economics.

www.pushpendramehta.com

pushpendramehtausa@gmail.com

Made in the USA
Middletown, DE
04 November 2020

23344170R00078